我的名是张欣恩
(GIMME CHANCE LEH)

我的名是张欣恩
(GIMME CHANCE LEH)

BY KRIS VANESSA TEO XIN-EN

PLAYWRIGHTS CANADA PRESS
TORONTO

First edition: October 2024
Printed and bound in Canada by Imprimerie Gauvin Ltée, Gatineau

Jacket art and design by Yeli Chuan
Author photo by Mike Tan

Playwrights Canada Press
202-269 Richmond St. W., Toronto, ON M5V 1X1
416.703.0013 | info@playwrightscanada.com | www.playwrightscanada.com

LIBRARY AND ARCHIVES CANADA CATALOGUING IN PUBLICATION
Title: Wo de ming shi Teo Xin En / Teo Xin En = Gimme chance leh / Kris Vanessa Teo Xin-En.
Other titles: Gimme chance leh
Names: Teo, Kris Vanessa Xin-En, author.
Description: Includes some text in Chinese, Malay, and Singlish.
Identifiers: Canadiana (print) 20240422651 | Canadiana (ebook) 2024042266X | ISBN 9780369105011 (softcover) | ISBN 9780369105028 (PDF) | ISBN 9780369105035 (EPUB)
Subjects: LCGFT: Drama.
Classification: LCC PS8639.E65 W6 2024 | DDC C812/.6—dc23

Playwrights Canada Press staff work across Turtle Island, on Treaty 7, Treaty 13, and Treaty 20 territories, which are the current and ancestral homes of the Anishinaabe Nations (Ojibwe / Chippewa, Odawa, Potawatomi, Algonquin, Saulteaux, Nipissing, and Mississauga / Michi Saagiig), the Blackfoot Confederacy (Kainai, Piikani, and Siksika), néhiyaw, Sioux, Stoney Nakoda, Tsuut'ina, Wendat, and members of the Haudenosaunee Confederacy (Mohawk, Oneida, Onondaga, Cayuga, Seneca, and Tuscarora), as well as Metis and Inuit peoples. It always was and always will be Indigenous land.

We acknowledge the financial support of the Canada Council for the Arts, the Ontario Arts Council (OAC), Ontario Creates, the Government of Ontario, and the Government of Canada for our publishing activities.

This play is dedicated to those whose lived experiences span
multitudes of
places,
cultures,
diaspora,
food,
languages,
dialects,
ways of thinking,
of feeling,
of singing,
of being.

All that you hold inside of you is magic. The wild and unabashed sounds that tumble out of your mouth when you speak is magic.

FOREWORD

Jenna Rodgers (she/her)

What does it mean to be a third-culture kid? I think of this term as referring to someone who spent a significant portion of their developmental years in a culture other than their own (which is to say, away from the culture of their parents or country of nationality). Typically we think of families whose parents work as missionaries, for the government, or for the military. We think of international schools and students in foreign countries learning English. As globalization has expanded and cities have become cultural melting pots, the label "cross-culture kids" has emerged, referring to children who share similarities with third-culture kids—they might be immigrants, have parents of different racial origins, or be an international adoptee.

Being raised in relationship to a third (or fourth or fifth) culture can bring many benefits—exposure to languages, a broader world view, cultural intelligence—but can also bring challenges that we are only just beginning to understand: a lack of attachment to a culture, a displaced sense of belonging, finding oneself "culturally homeless." I'm barely scratching the surface of this topic—as you can imagine, much research has been done on the social psychology of being raised in the liminal spaces between cultures, but I believe this liminal space is what drew me to Kris's story.

This play is clearly based on Kris's lived experiences. She was born in Canada to ethnically Chinese Singaporean parents, and moved to Singapore as a young child, where she spent her adolescence before returning to Canada for post-secondary education. Due to cultural blending and the multitude of languages present in Singapore, her Chinese family primarily spoke English at home, which inadvertently distanced her from her extended family and proved to be a rarity in a country where the norm is to be educated in English but speak another language (or two!) at home. So is Kris a third-culture kid, or a cross-culture kid? Hard to say, but both concepts gesture toward her lived experience of what the CBC Digital Original audio play of 我的名是张欣恩 *(Gimme chance leh)* aptly called "cultural whiplash."

Much of what she addresses feels deeply resonant to me: a wholly Canadian born-and-raised biracial kid whose family backgrounds are so different from one another I took for granted the intercultural education I was inadvertently receiving simply by existing. My mother is Chinese and my father is Welsh, and despite the well-meaning assumption that most people have, Mom was actually born in Canada, while Dad was born in Great Britain. He migrated as a child as his parents sought a new life in Sherwood Park, Alberta, in the 1950s. Mom was born and raised in the Edmonton area, living in a handful of suburbs, including Stony Plain and Fort Saskatchewan, always in relationship to the convenience store or other business that her parents operated.

The second oldest of six, she didn't grow up speaking or reading English and struggled in school until the third grade, when she says the language finally clicked. She went on to become an English major at the University of Alberta, which is where she met my dad. They ultimately decided to raise me and my sister in English for practical reasons. It was a language they could both speak and understand—it was more practical than the ever-diminishing Toisan dialect that Mom's family speaks.

As an adult I'm conscious of this absence in my life—though I certainly don't fault my parents for their choice. It feels like I'm disconnected from some mysterious way of understanding my own Chineseness. And yes, I could go out and learn Chinese, though learning Toisan is difficult these days (it's easy to get seduced by the more practical Mandarin or by loyalty to my maternal grandmother's Cantonese mother tongue). My relationship to Chineseness is deeply Canadian. My Chinese ancestors have been in so-called Canada on and off since the late 1800s, most born in China and then arriving through marriage once the head tax lifted. I have more Chinese ancestors buried in the land on this continent than I do White ancestors. My Chineseness is known through the foods my grandmother and mother would prepare for our family, and the distinctly Chinese Canadian prairie food that they would prepare for the small-town restaurant and bar my grandparents owned before they retired.

I have come to know the cultures of my ancestries in different ways, and I look upon it as my own distinct sort of culture. Perhaps we all have these? The culture of your family, made of your personal experiences, the places you've lived, and the foods you've eaten: a culture shaped by the way you've navigated the world. I think this is what's kept me drawn to 我的名是张欣恩 *(Gimme chance leh)* since its inception.

Kris brought me onto this project in 2018 as a collaborator with Chromatic Theatre. We had intended to premiere a full production in 2020. (Hah! We were mid-rehearsal when the great pause began.) At the time I was Artistic Director of Chromatic Theatre and was just finishing up my Artistic Leadership Residency with the National Theatre School of Canada. I had spent a good portion of 2019 travelling across Canada and then to Australia to specifically think about theatre and our industry's relationship to colonization. I was really holding on to some frustration about working in a geographically large country that doesn't have much infrastructure for touring (and what little we have tends to be concentrated in Quebec, Ontario, and British Columbia), limiting our opportunities to really understand our national theatre ecology. Festivals have been slowly atrophying—Magnetic North and the playRites Festival had both come and gone, and our opportunities to gather were dwindling (little did I know what the pandemic would have in store). And people kept asking me why I was in Alberta. Why would I move here? How could I live here? Isn't this a place where artists of colour leave?

And I desperately wanted that narrative to change.

Alberta can be a challenging place to create art, but in many ways that is what makes it more rewarding. People leave because there are even fewer opportunities to see themselves represented on stage—and isn't that even more of a reason to tell our stories? To let people know that not only do BIPOC folks exist on the prairies, but we are making cool art with themes that resonate globally.

When the performing arts ground to a halt in March 2020, 我的名是张欣恩 *(Gimme chance leh)* was mid-rehearsal. And while Chromatic Theatre tried valiantly to get the full production up, it just wasn't in the cards. We were, however, able to produce a full audio play through the CBC's Digital Originals, a program that called for online content during the pandemic. This option allowed us to honour and expand upon the work of our incredible sound designer Thomas Geddes (another biracial artist!). Thomas stepped into the director's chair to create a full audio version of the show—which can still be found online at www.cbc.ca/player/play/audio/1.5840682. I am excited to see it performed live one day—perhaps with Kris as the performer, but perhaps not. I believe that the themes of this play transcend the individual who wrote it, which is why I programmed it and why I continue to advocate for it.

我的名是张欣恩 *(Gimme chance leh)* is not *just* a pandemic play. It was programmed pre-pandemic, and the iterations that came out during the pandemic are a love letter to racialized artists who are wondering if it is worthwhile to tell their story. The answer is yes, it is always worthwhile. Someone out there needs to hear it. Institutions need to be challenged to engage with the diasporic, to put our languages on stage, to reach the hundreds of thousands of new Canadians who would be happy to see theatre that they could understand.

Way back when Kris first started writing this play and I was serving more as a dramaturg than as a director, I asked her who she was writing for. This was a question we often revisited. And the answer changed. Maybe it is still changing. You see, this play isn't specifically *for* Singaporean Canadians raised in Calgary and Singapore—that's what it's *about*. The play is *for* anyone who speaks multiple languages on a daily basis, for anyone who finds themselves code-switching between home and school, for anyone who struggles to keep up with the complex social coding of middle school, and so much more. It is an investigation of how people are shaped by both the culture we live in and the culture of our families. It is a beautiful act of storytelling, and ripe with opportunities to engage with creative collaborators.

I hope you enjoy reading this play as much as I enjoyed working on it. I hope you experience moments of cultural dissonance or confusion. If you can't understand Mandarin, don't worry—most of the audiences that see the play won't understand it either, so take some solace in experiencing the disconnect that Kris is replaying from her own youth! And if you decide you want to produce this play (hooray!), I encourage you to look for collaborators locally. Maybe you already know how to speak Mandarin, but if you don't, I guarantee you there are a plethora of professional artists who identify as third-culture or biracial or multilingual who would not only happily work on the play and bring their own experiences, but would also happily help you find the Mandarin speaker you need.

Canada is getting more diverse, and it is imperative that storytellers and theatre artists continue to practise working across difference. Theatre is inherently collaborative, which is a major part of *why* I'm drawn to it as an art form. Our craft is to find the heart of a story, to bring it to life, and share it with captive audiences. Our practice necessitates studying humanity, and as the populations in our urban centres shift, so too should we be striving to understand the value of stories that extend beyond our personal lived experiences. We can only grow as theatre artists when we're in relationship with other people, and meaningful collaboration requires a depth of connection. As a director and a dramaturg, I am constantly studying and practising ways of communicating with a myriad of artists. I must strive to listen deeply, to communicate clearly, and to dream broadly: all skills I began to develop early in my life thanks to my own intercultural upbringing.

Jenna Rodgers (she/her) is a mixed-race, Treaty 7–based director and dramaturg. She is Artistic Director of Concrete Theatre, Founding Artistic Director of Chromatic Theatre, and served as Dramaturg for the Playwrights Lab at the Banff Centre for Arts and Creativity for over ten years. Jenna is Board Co-Chair of the Literary Managers and Dramaturgs of the Americas and Director of Theatre Alberta's Artstrek Program. She is a passionate advocate for equity in the arts, a fierce supporter of new play development, and is learning to raise small responsible humans while maintaining a career in the arts.

AUTHOR'S PREFACE

When I started writing 我的名是张欣恩 *(Gimme chance leh)* in 2016, I was feeling so far away from myself and so deeply lonely. Ironically, it was because I was lonely that I had spent my first four years back in Calgary distancing myself from everything that culturally made me who I am.

I wasn't the *only* person of colour in my undergrad program, but it was still a dominantly white space—something that was completely new to me . . . and to be quite honest, maybe it was even something that an old version of myself used to be excited about because of all the perceived privileges of being adjacent to whiteness.

I always have the desire to connect deeply with people, but no matter how good I was at code switching, people would notice the little differences in how I embodied my upbringing in Singapore and hang on to these differences as if they were the only things to know about me. Whatever I had to share about myself to someone would always be secondary to the fact that I was foreign to them. Everything authentic about me felt silenced and invisible.

Whoever I was back then didn't have the self-esteem to know that my worth as a person wasn't dependent on these white people being interested to know me, and that maybe they were the ones who weren't worth being in my orbit. Sometimes, I still think about what I used to value as a new immigrant and am harsh on who I used to be. I hate and cringe at the choices I made in order to protect myself. I often feel like I betrayed myself, but I'm also learning to hold space for myself as someone who can grow, change my mind, and shift accordingly.

My best and most generous self has so much empathy, curiosity, and care for who I used to be. She was just trying her best with what she knew then, surviving the way she best knew how.

She just wanted to be seen. I love her so much. I've since been on a journey of coming home to myself, to find ease in existing in my body however, wherever I am. I've been working on letting go of trying to control myself. Whatever I sound like today, in this moment, with this word, is whatever I sound like. It might be expressed differently tomorrow. I don't need to curate the expression of myself to be worth being seen, held and celebrated. Neither do you.

It's taken me years to arrive where I am now and I'm not done yet. I will likely be on this journey for the rest of my life. I hope that whoever you are, you read this play and are moved to exist in a way that creates the kind of comfort and safety that allows others to lean into being themselves fully. And if you are a racialized person, I hope 我的名是张欣恩 *(Gimme chance leh)* inspires you to come home to yourself. And I want you to know that whatever way, scale, and pace you choose to do that is valid, worthwhile, and a gift that you are so worth giving yourself. This play is my gift to you.

我的名是张欣恩 *(Gimme chance leh)* was scheduled to be first produced by Chromatic Theatre at the Motel Theatre, Calgary, from March 25 to April 4, 2020, but was cancelled because of the onset of the COVID-19 pandemic. It was to feature the following cast and creative team:

Performer: Kris Vanessa Teo Xin-En (张欣恩)

Artistic Director/Director: Jenna Rodgers
Production Manager: Michael Luong
Lighting Designer/Costume Designer: Bianca Guimarães de Manuel
Set Designer: Sarah Uwadiae
Projection Designer: Tori Morrison
Technical Director/Sound Designer: Thomas Geddes
Stage Manager: Jennifer Yeung

The play was later produced as a CBC Digital Original in 2020 with the following audio production team:

Performer: Kris Vanessa Teo Xin-En (张欣恩)
Co-Directors: Jenna Rodgers and Thomas Geddes
Assistant Director: Jesse Del Fierro
Sound Designer and Mixer: Thomas Geddes

You can listen to the audio play now by following this QR code:

A revised version of the play, 我的名是张欣恩 *(Gimme chance leh) Redux: A Team Together*, was produced by Chromatic Theatre, supported by Vertigo Theatre's Agency Residency Program, from May 22 to June 5, 2021. This was a film project presented online of the creative culmination of the artists, designers, and production members collaborating digitally over the span of two weeks to allow a peek behind the scenes of the different iterations of the original live production. As a collective, the artists ruminate on the themes of the play, reminisce on the process, and reflect on how they and their families came to find a home in Alberta.

Cinematographer, Director, and Sound Designer: Thomas Geddes
Performer: Kris Vanessa Teo Xin-En (张欣恩)
B Camera Operator and Editor: Kara Artym
Assistant Director: Jesse Del Fierro
Technical Director and Assistant Sound Designer: Daniela Fernandez
Stage Manager: Sadaf Ganji
Lighting Designer and Costume Designer: Bianca Guimarães de Manuel
Set Designer: Sarah Uwadiae
Projection Designer: Tori Morrison

KRIS: *(with a Canadian accent)* Migration—the movement of people from one place to another, with the intention of settling in a new location. This movement is usually motivated by work and wanting to build a better life. There was a time when the Chinese were concentrated solely in China. Our population grew from 50 million in the first century to about 400 million in the 19th century, which was when we started leaving China in large numbers in search of wealth in faraway places. At first, many of us migrated to nearby Asian countries like Korea, Japan, Myanmar, Cambodia, Laos, Thailand, and Vietnam. Smaller numbers left for Africa, Latin America, and India. Then, an ever-growing group started moving to the West. Like my parents. I was born here in Moh'kins'tsis (Calgary), but was raised in Singapore and moved back here, where the Bow River meets the Elbow River, to settle. I am a settler of this land. I would like to acknowledge that we live, thrive, and continue to grow our roots on the traditional territories of the people of the Treaty 7 region in Southern Alberta, which includes the Blackfoot Confederacy, comprising the Siksika, Piikani, and Kainai First Nations, as well as the Tsuut'ina First Nation, and the Îyârhe Nakoda, including the Chiniki, Bearspaw, and Goodstoney First Nations. The city of Calgary is also home to Districts 5 and 6 of the Métis Nation of Alberta's Battle River Territory. I am thankful to now call Moh'kins'tsis my home.

Singapore is also home to me. Singapore, Singapura, 新加坡, சிங்கப்பூர். As a Singaporean Chinese woman, I want to acknowledge that the Malay people are the indigenous people of Singapore. Singapore is a multiracial, multi-religious and multilingual country, with English as its lingua franca. It is home to mostly Chinese, Malay, and Indian people. Although dominant in numbers and privilege, Chinese people are also settlers of the land, myself included. Singapore is a clean, wealthy, and modern country and I am thankful for the safety and comforts of a country that developed so rapidly. But I also want to acknowledge that prioritizing the English language has led to the gradual erasure of a multitude of dialects. Singapore used to have a thriving jungle of languages, pruned down to only four official ones—English, Chinese, Malay, and Tamil. People like my grandparents, whose only languages are their ancestral dialects—like Teochew and Cantonese, are disconnected from their English-educated descendants. People like me. But, to ensure our success as a newly independent nation, sacrifices had to be made.

KRIS waves to the audience.

大家你好!

She points to herself.

我的名是张欣恩。

She picks an audience member and points to them as she asks them a question.

你叫什么名?

KRIS pauses for a moment to wait for a response. She points back to herself and repeats slowly.

我的名是张欣恩。

KRIS points back to the audience member she is speaking to.

你叫什么名?

KRIS points back to herself and shortens her sentence, hoping that she is easier to understand.

张欣恩。

Again, KRIS points back to the audience member she is speaking to.

你呢?

KRIS repeats this until someone understands that this is a greeting and an exchange of names. When they offer their name back to KRIS, *she repeats it back for everyone to hear.*

(insert name), 你好！

KRIS *repeats this process of greeting and exchanging names with three to five other audience members.*

Wha! 你们全部都超越我对你们理解华语的期望。

Suddenly, KRIS *switches to speaking English in a Canadian accent.*

Wow! That was really great! All of you were keeping up while I was speaking Chinese! On a scale of one to ten, with one being the worst and ten being the best, how good do you think my Chinese is?

KRIS *pauses to wait for a response, someone to answer, and accepts whatever answers she receives.*

In Singapore, English is our first language. In school, all of our lessons are taught in English, but we also take what we call Mother Tongue Lessons. Singapore is a multicultural country made up of mostly Chinese, Malay, and Indian people. During Mother Tongue Lessons, we break up into our racial groups and learn our mother tongues. I ALWAYS DREADED IT. Because . . . *(depending on the audience's response earlier on)* you guessed right/wrong . . . I was TERRIBLE at Chinese.

A hunger pang hits KRIS *in the gut.*

Wow, I am starving!

Kris snaps her fingers. THE CHICKEN RICE UNCLE *"appears."* KRIS *switches from speaking English to Singlish.*

(in Singlish) Uncle! I want one plate of chicken rice!

THE CHICKEN RICE UNCLE *doesn't realize* KRIS *is Chinese and responds to her in Malay instead.*

THE CHICKEN RICE UNCLE: *(in Malay)* Satu? Nasi ayam?

KRIS: Err . . . Uncle, 我是华人。

THE CHICKEN RICE UNCLE: Eh?? 我以为你是马来人, 你的皮肤很黑。

He laughs.

Okay! 你要吃什么?

KRIS: Umm, 给我一盘鸡饭!

THE CHICKEN RICE UNCLE: Okay 你要烧鸡还是要白鸡?

KRIS: 烧鸡还是白鸡? . . .

THE CHICKEN RICE UNCLE is impatient.

THE CHICKEN RICE UNCLE: 快点！还有其他人！

KRIS: *(flustered)* Uhhh . . . 我要白鸡饭！

THE CHICKEN RICE UNCLE: Orh . . . okay!!

KRIS turns away in relief, but THE CHICKEN RICE UNCLE calls out to her again.

THE CHICKEN RICE UNCLE: Eh 小妹你的鸡饭要鸡腿肉还是鸡胸肉?!

KRIS: . . . Huuuh??? 我要一盘白鸡饭！

THE CHICKEN RICE UNCLE: 对啦！鸡腿还是鸡胸?!?!

KRIS: Huh?? . . . Uncle . . . 我听不懂 . . .

THE CHICKEN RICE UNCLE: AIYOH!! 你刚才不是讲你是华人meh? I thought you Chinese??

KRIS is offended. She snaps her fingers and THE CHICKEN RICE UNCLE is gone.

KRIS: 华人就是华人！我可以证明我的华语能力是不错的！来，我们一起玩一个游戏看看你可以跟得上我吗?不用怕，这个游戏很好玩！

KRIS picks an audience member to play a clapping game from her childhood that is kind of a combination of patty cake and rock-paper-scissors. She teaches them the game slowly and patiently.

来, 跟我玩, 好不好?我们上, 我们下, 我们后前走, 我们一二三, 我们四五六, 我们七八九, 我们好朋友, 我们cherry cherry, lom jiam pass pass pass!

If KRIS doesn't win the game, she might cheat to win. When she wins the game, she is triumphant and gloats about it in a silly childlike way. KRIS plays the game with three to five audience members.

哈!我赢了!这个游戏很好玩对不对?如果我的华语那么差, 我怎么会玩这个游戏?我不只会讲华语, 我也会写中文字!今天, 你会学习怎么写中文字。关于华语, 我通常是学生。但现在, 你们是学生, 我是你们的老师。你可以叫我张老师。我要教你怎么写我的名字: 张欣恩。你应该可以在你的座位下找到一些纸和笔。大家来!

As KRIS is speaking, she gestures to the audience that they can find paper and pens under their seats. Then, she goes through how to write the strokes of her Chinese name via the overhead projector with the audience as they follow along on their pieces of paper.

heng zhe, heng, shu, heng zhe gou, heng, shu gou, pie, na—Zhang pie, pie, heng, shu, pie, heng gou, pie, na—Xin

shu, heng zhe, heng, pie, na, heng, dian, wan gou, dian, dian—En

Zhang Xin-En!

(with a Canadian accent) Now, I want to know about you. When you were in school and about to start your exam, what's the first thing you had to do?

> KRIS *pauses for the audience to respond.*

Right! You have to write your name! And you know what? I forgot how to write my Chinese name. My mind went blank for a while, because . . . how was I going to answer the actual exam questions if I didn't know how to write my name?? Think, Kris!!!

Think!!! What are you going to do?!! OH!! I raise my hand. "Ms. Tan! I have to blow my nose . . . can I go get some tissue from my bag?" She believed me! So, I went out of my classroom to where my bag was to sneak a peek at the cover of my Chinese textbook, where my mother had faithfully written my Chinese name.

> KRIS *approaches someone in the audience to borrow their sheet of paper from when they learnt how to write her name.* KRIS *memorizes the strokes to write her name in a frenzy before returning the paper back to the audience member.*

heng zhe, heng, shu, heng zhe gou, heng, shu gou, pie, na—Zhang

pie, pie, heng, shu, pie, heng gou, pie, na—Xin

shu, heng zhe, heng, pie, na, heng, dian, wan gou, dian, dian—En

ZHANG. XIN. EN. Hah!!!!!!

(with a Canadian accent) Did I get an A for my Chinese exam? No. But did I pass? OF COURSE, I DID! All my mother needed to be happy was a C, because in my family, C is for Celebrate! C is also for Cantonese, which my mother grew up speaking. Cantonese is my mother's mother tongue. She also speaks Singlish. When I first moved to Singapore, I remember asking my mother, "Everyone in Singapore is speaking English, but it sounds different from me. How do I speak that way?"

KRIS'S MOTHER: *(in Singlish)* Orhhhhh . . . you mean Singlish ah? You just add the sound "la" and "lor" at the end of your sentence lor! Liddat can already lor!

KRIS: *(with a Canadian accent)* Everyone in Singapore kept saying I sounded so Canadian. I didn't feel like I belonged in Singapore. I wanted that sense of belonging, *(switches to Singlish)* so I talk liddat lah. So people don't think I trying to be better than them or what la. Singlish words ah is a mix of Chinese, Malay, Tamil, British English, and Chinese dialects like Hokkien, Teochew, and Cantonese. I tell you ah, everyone in Singapore knows it budden ah not everyone speak it.

Because nowsadays ah, if you speak a lot of Singlish in professional settings ah, people will think you low class or uneducated. The gahment, they dun like their citizens to speak Singlish. *(switches to Canadian accent)* In fact, they created an annual Speak Good English Movement to encourage Singaporeans to speak in a way that commands global respect. *(switches to Singlish)* So I can talk like dis la! *(switches to Canadian accent)* But when the moment calls for it, I can speak like this. I mean, why wouldn't I want to get ahead? English is my first language, and I'm good at it! I moved to Singapore as a child, sounding like an *(in Singlish)* "ang moh" *(with a Canadian accent)* who liked to *(in Singlish)* "jiak kantang"! Does anyone know what "ang moh" is? Can anyone guess?

> *KRIS waits for the audience to guess, and she entertains their guesses.*

(in Singlish) So "ang" is a Hokkien word that means red, and "mo" is another Hokkien word that means hair. So red hair! "Ang moh," the literal translation means red hair! And what about "jiak kantang"? Anybody want to guess again?

> *Again, KRIS waits for the audience to guess, and entertains their guesses.*

(in Singlish) Yes/No! "Jiak" is a Hokkien word that means "to eat" and "kantang" actually is come from the Malay word

"kentang" which means potato. So, to the people in Singapore ah, all of you white people are the people with red hair, who like to eat potato!!

> KRIS *laughs wildly.*

(with a Canadian accent) I grew up speaking English at home. So, the language I tried making friends with in school was always English. Chinese was such an awkward and uncomfortable language for me to be around. And even though we all knew English, many of my peers grew up speaking their mother tongues at home with their families. I wanted to sit and laugh with them and be a part of their inside jokes. I wanted friends to pass secret notes to in class—but there was no one to do all that with in English. But before long, I met Nicole and Joanne. We were all terrible at speaking Chinese. Suddenly, I had my own little group of friends—and FINALLY in a language I understood.

> KRIS *breaks out into a silly rhyme from her childhood and claps along:*

(in Singlish) O Pillar! Caterpillar! Lazy boy! Sexy girl! Ping pong! Sing song! Go to school! Play a fool!

> KRIS *says the rhyme a second time, but faster.*

O Pillar! Caterpillar! Lazy boy! Sexy girl! Ping pong! Sing song! Go to school! Play a fool!

(with a Canadian accent) Anyone who seemed "too Chinese" for us, we called them "cheena" behind their backs. The word cheena is a derogatory term used by Singaporeans, even Chinese Singaporeans, to mock anyone who has any association with mainland China. Chinese people mocking other Chinese people for being "too Chinese." We didn't have interest in getting to know anyone who spoke Chinese. It's not like I knew enough Chinese to start any friendships with cheena people anyway. But it's okay. They weren't the cool kids. We were. If a classmate pronounced a word that sounded Singlish, we'd repeat it among ourselves and laugh ourselves silly.

(laughs and then switches to Singlish) Tell me abourit? *(switches back to Canadian accent)* Hey, it's pronounced "about it," not "abourit." If you don't start saying it right, we aren't going to stop laughing. Fix your pronunciation.

> KRIS *laughs in a mean way.*

(with a Canadian accent) All of us who spoke English really well formed an exclusive group of friends. We had a spot in school where only we were allowed to sit. We were the shiiiiit—twelve-year-old English-speaking elites.

> *As* KRIS *tells the following story, she is crushing up some Mamee Monster noodles, tearing the bag open, fishing out the packet of seasoning, dumping it in with the noodles, holding the bag closed, and shaking up the bag to mix the seasoning in.*

(with a Canadian accent) One time, we were sitting in our usual spot and Zhi Hao, who wasn't part of the group, walked by. He was eating Mamee Monster noodles. He stopped, and in his broken English, offered us some. Free snacks!!! My favourite!! So, I stick my fingers into the bag and I grab a handful. But Nicole politely declined, and suddenly I felt like I had touched something dirty. When Zhi Hao walked away, Nicole whispered to me, "That was disgusting. I saw him lick the seasoning off his fingers and he put that same hand back into the bag before he offered it to us!!! Ugh gross. Typical cheena." I immediately felt a red wave of shame wash over me. Nicole thought he was disgusting, but what did she think of ME putting my own hands in his disgusting bag of Mamee Monster noodles? AND enjoying it? What did she think of me now? Does she think I am disgusting and cheena too? Is she still going to be my friend?

> *Wanting to comfort herself with some food,* KRIS *snaps her fingers.* THE CHICKEN RICE UNCLE *appears.*

Uncle, 我的鸡饭好了吗?

THE CHICKEN RICE UNCLE: *(impatiently)* 鸡腿肉还是鸡胸肉?

> KRIS *is silent. Maybe she repeats the words to herself, but she still can't answer the question because she doesn't understand.* THE CHICKEN RICE UNCLE *clues into this.*

Aiyoh! 你还是听不懂?

KRIS: 听不懂。

THE CHICKEN RICE UNCLE: 哎呀, 来, Uncle 教你。

KRIS: Orh.

Different parts of a cooked chicken are being projected as THE CHICKEN RICE UNCLE explains to KRIS what they are called in Chinese.

THE CHICKEN RICE UNCLE: 鸡腿。这个是鸡腿。鸡。腿。

KRIS: OHHHHHH!! 鸡腿!

THE CHICKEN RICE UNCLE: 然后, 这个是鸡胸。鸡。胸。

KRIS: Ohhhh! 鸡胸。

THE CHICKEN RICE UNCLE: Ahhh 对, 你明白吗?

KRIS: 明白!

THE CHICKEN RICE UNCLE: 所以, 你要哪一个?

KRIS: . . . huh . . . Uncle . . . 我两个都不要!只有那两个吗?

THE CHICKEN RICE UNCLE: 哇, 你不会自己跟我讲but 你那么挑剔!

Feeling defeated, KRIS *turns to walk away. But* THE CHICKEN RICE UNCLE *calls her back.*

跟你开玩笑而已啦!回来!Okay, 你不要鸡腿肉, 你也不要鸡胸肉, 你到底要吃什么?

KRIS: Uhhh . . . 我想吃鸡用来飞的身体部位!

THE CHICKEN RICE UNCLE: 哦, 你想要鸡翅膀!

Chicken wings are projected as THE CHICKEN RICE UNCLE *understands what* KRIS *wants.*

KRIS: 对对对!鸡翅膀!

THE CHICKEN RICE UNCLE: 你的要求很高leh!

KRIS *laughs. She snaps her fingers and* THE CHICKEN RICE UNCLE *is gone.*

KRIS: *(with a Canadian accent)* Being good at English helped me maintain a semblance of elite status in Singapore. It meant no one would think I was cheena. If I'm so good at speaking English and so bad at speaking Chinese, Canada is going to be perfect for me, because you speak English here . . . don't you? But when I moved here, I realised I was far from elite. I could only be a cool Asian. Or a fobby Asian—you know, fresh off the boat. Whatever it is, I am always Asian.

GENERIC COLONIZER WHITE PERSON: WOW! You're Chinese?

You don't sound like you're from China! How long have you been learning English for?

KRIS: . . . I'm from Singapore and English is our first language.

GENERIC COLONIZER WHITE PERSON: That's amazing! You're not like those Asians. Those fobby ones. I wish they would just learn to speak the language of the place they're going to migrate to you know?

KRIS: When I don't stand up for myself or for the Asian people you've met and feel compelled to tell me about, it's pretty easy to slide under your radar as a cool Asian. I'll admit, many times, I've just taken the easier route by smiling and agreeing with what you're saying. In fact, I know hearing a westernized accent is more palatable for Canadians, so even if you can't see it, I'm translating between languages and accents in my head at high speed, so that when I speak, you don't feel uncomfortable and alienate me. Most of the time, I do a good job, but if I let my guard down, or I have to speak or read words I've never heard in a Canadian accent before, it feels like a power outage happens in my brain. It's too much data *(pronounced day-ta)* for me to process. WAIT. WHICH COUNTRY AM I IN?? WHAT ACCENT SHOULD I USE???

GENERIC COLONIZER WHITE PERSON: "Data?" *(pronounced day-ta)* You mean data? *(pronounced deh-ta)*

KRIS: Yes, data *(pronounced deh-ta)*, sorry! Let's get in the queue before it gets too long!!

GENERIC COLONIZER WHITE PERSON: Queue??? Kris, are you talking about the line? *(laughing)* What??? An Asian girl going all British on me? *(continues laughing)*

KRIS: Well, Singapore was colonized by the British.

GENERIC COLONIZER WHITE PERSON: *(confused)* What?

KRIS: Nothing.

GENERIC COLONIZER WHITE PERSON: What did you say? I didn't catch that.

KRIS: Singapore was colonized by the British. *(awkward silence)* Sorry, it's my fault, I'm really running amok *(pronounced uh-mock)* here with all my terrible pronunciations.

GENERIC COLONIZER WHITE PERSON: *(laughing)* Kris, it's pronounced UH-MUCK, not UH-MOCK. If you don't start saying it right, we aren't going to stop laughing. Fix your pronunciation.

KRIS: Oh! Sorry! Okay! Yes, I'll fix it. Wait, what? People are laughing?? Please don't laugh. Sorry sorry sorry sorry, I'm not as fobby as I seem, I was actually born here. Don't look at me, just pretend you didn't hear me speak with my gross Singlish accent. I don't usually speak that way. Yes yes yes yes yes please correct me oh my god stop stop stop stop stop stop stop laughing at me don't laugh at me I'm not cheena okay!

KRIS snaps out of her panic. It's like waking up from a nightmare.

(with a Canadian accent) I can't remember when it started happening but one day speaking Chinese suddenly became cool. I think it was when Nicole and Joanne started hanging out with the prettiest, most popular girls in our school. They were twins. Double the height, double the skinniness, double the big round eyes, and the never-ending length of straight hair. But I didn't look like that. It felt like Nicole and Joanne were starting to spend more time with them and not with me. Sometimes I'd be invited to come along, but that started to dwindle. I was also confused because the twins were as Chinese-speaking as they came. In fact, they were the epitome of what being cheena was. Maybe because all the boys had crushes on the twins. Maybe looks were more important than being cheena or not. And now, even Nicole and Joanne were speaking Chinese!! I just . . . can't understand why it used to be that if anyone else did anything that might be cheena, we would make fun of them and not be friends with them. But when Nicole and Joanne change their minds and decide they like speaking Chinese it's totally okay?? Why do they get to dictate the rules? What about the people we used to make fun of? Were they okay to be around now, and I was out? I thought we were going to be best friends for life, but I was alone on the last day of primary school.

And now we all went to new secondary schools. I was half anxious and half excited for a clean slate. I wanted new friends so badly I think I was willing to do anything. Except . . . in my new school, the cool kids spoke Chinese.

KRIS groans in frustration.

It was the first week of secondary school. I heard loud whispers and giggles coming from behind me. I turned to look and saw a group of older girls from the class sitting next to mine, laughing softly amongst themselves over some inside joke they were having. They were the cool older girls. As I was walking to my classroom that morning, I felt a tap on my shoulder. I turned around. It was that same group of girls! They asked me to follow them. New friends! I was so excited I was practically skipping. I ended up in a quiet corner of the school. As I looked at these girls I wanted to be friends with, something inside me shifted, and I became hyperaware that I was alone with them.

GIRL: *(in Singlish)* Eh chiobu 你是Vanessa ah?

KRIS: *(with a Canadian accent)* Oh yeah, I went by my middle name in secondary school. I just imagined "Vanessa" was closer to what a popular white girl would be named.

GIRL: *(in Singlish)* Eh chiobu 你是Vanessa ah?

KRIS nods her head.

你看我的朋友不爽啊?

KRIS: Huh??

GIRL: 你看我的朋友不爽啊?她跟我说你屌她。

KRIS: *(with a Canadian accent)* I still don't understand what they're saying. But I awkwardly try to converse with them anyway. Uhhh . . . 我没有看过她!对不起!我不认识她! *(in Singlish)* I dunno what you're talking about.

GIRL: 她跟我说你屌她。You dun lie okay. 你屌她对不对?你不爽啊chiobu?

KRIS: *(with a Canadian accent)* My inability to understand this fully seemed to anger them even more.

GIRL: 下次你见到她时, 你最好对她微笑。如果她跟我讲你屌她多一次, 你走出去这个学校时候, 我们全部会来打你。你听懂吗chiobu?

KRIS: *(with a Canadian accent)* I didn't understand a single word that was being said even though I kind of knew it couldn't be good things. After they walked away, I pulled the one person I knew aside. Within the privacy of the closest bathroom stall, she explained that the word "chiobu" was a Hokkien word to describe an attractive girl and that it was being used ironically on me.

The shame of hearing that explained to me by someone I wanted to like me burned so hot it was impossible to control that prickly, wet feeling in my eyes. She looked at me like

. . . like how did I not understand something so simple—I was scum to those older girls. She was right though. I didn't understand and my perfect English wasn't helping. From that moment, I made a conscious decision to take my perfect English and break it all up.

(in Singlish) I tell you ah, I know Singlish ah, the English is like not 100% correct one. But now at my new school, I don't just speak the heavy Singlish, I purposely speak the very broken English one. When I talk in school ah, I don't let people know I can speak English well one. I pretend like imma chao ah lian. Or I try to talk Chinese. But you all already know what. My Chinese cannot make it one! Anyone who make me angry ah . . . "WHA KANINABEH CHAO CHEE BYE AH!!!! 要死啊你?! FARK YOU ASSHO!!!!" I change the way I talk so much in the end those girls still don't like me. They just leave me alone la. I mean, I oso dun like myself. Dun recognize myself oso. For the first two years in that school ah, those girls that threaten me ah, they also threaten the girls in my class not to talk to me. Everyone scared of them . . . so of course they bo pian don't talk to me la! If I am them, I also won't talk to me lor. Then got some girls in my class, they want the older girls to like them, want to go the extra mile . . . so they start to bully me oso. When I am in school, I try to be tough, keep my face angry, so even if people don't want to talk to me, they know: I OSO DOWAN TO TALK TO THEM OKAY. Tiring leh. After school when I go home. I just feel like going to sleep sia. I don't study. I don't do my homework. Sometimes I just don't go to school. Too sian to get out of bed. Wish I could sleep forever. It felt like forever I am just

wrapped in this blanket of darkness. So . . . my mom brought me out for my favourite chilli crab meal. Because she knows when I'm down, good food always makes me feel damn shiok.

KRIS pauses to ask the audience a question.

(with a Canadian accent) Do you want to hear more about . . . chilli crabs?

KRIS waits for the audience to say yes. Even if they say no, she tells them anyway.

(in Singlish) Chilli crab is a signature Singaporean dish. We usually wait for the crabs to get cooked in this thick sauce that is savoury, sweet, and spicy all at the same time, and it has small pieces of crab meat mixed inside the sauce, but the most important part is that the WHOLE CRAB is in the sauce. And the best way to eat it ah is to just use your hands. You use your bare hands to crack the shell and suck the crab meat and sauce out of the shell. Everyone's favourite part is the pincer because it has the most meat. There is usually so much sauce. There's so much sauce until sometimes ah you just scoop and drink like is a soup liddat. And most of the time right, chilli crab is serve with 炸馒头, which are these small square pieces of bread that is deep fried. It got a crispy outer shell, and when you bite inside ah, the inside is soft and chewy bread. We use the 炸馒头as a vehicle to get as much sauce as you can from the bowl into your mouth. Eat until vehhh shiok!!!! But to me ah, it is not as yummy as roṭi prata. Roti prata is a soft and chewy flatbread that starts as a round piece of dough, and

then the roti prata uncle takes the dough and spins it and flips it and folds it round and round again and again. And then if you wan ah he can crack an egg inside. Den, he will spin it and flip it and fold it again until got so many soft stretchy layers. And then you can dip it in fish or mutton curry. Or can put sugar oso. My favourite is the fish curry. I dun usually like the sugar with my roti prata but you know what I like sugar in? Putu mayam! Putu mayam is this rice noodle pancake that is steamed with pandan leaves so it has this super fragrant smell, and you tear off pieces of the pancake and use it to pick up a mix of grated coconut and this BRIGHT orange sugar. My father always buy putu mayam for me for breakfast when I go back Singapore to visit. Wha you see, I only just talking about my favourite food but I oredi feel better. And hungrier! I cannot wait to makan!

Excited to order more food, KRIS *snaps her fingers.* THE CHICKEN RICE UNCLE *appears.*

Uncle ah, 刚才, 我要白鸡饭, 只有鸡翅膀好像不够。我可以加肉吗?

THE CHICKEN RICE UNCLE: 这样麻烦leh你。Okay 快点, 你要什么?

KRIS: Hmmm, 我要白鸡胸肉。EH! 不是不是不是, sorry!! 不是鸡胸, 我想要的是鸡腿肉!

THE CHICKEN RICE UNCLE: 你confirm 吗?

KRIS: Confirm, guarantee plus chop! 我的鸡腿肉不要骨。Oh 还可以加uhhh. 鸡uhhh. Liver?

THE CHICKEN RICE UNCLE: 什么来的?

KRIS: 是在鸡的身体里面的??

THE CHICKEN RICE UNCLE laughs at this description, but understands.

THE CHICKEN RICE UNCLE: Ohhhh 你要鸡肝是不是?

Chicken liver gets projected as KRIS learns the Chinese words for it.

KRIS: 对!鸡肝!

THE CHICKEN RICE UNCLE: 很好, 你等一下!

KRIS: Orh!

KRIS snaps her fingers and THE CHICKEN RICE UNCLE disappears.

(in Singlish) For a few years, everyday show up to school wif no friends very difficult for me. Everyday I feel like shit. In my final year, I kena assigned by the teacher to sit in the back corner of my class with two Chinese speaking girls—Hui Ting and Cheryl. Sian. Why they don't ask me to sit next to Malay or Indian people? Even if end up I don't like them, at

least can speak English what! Budden hor, when you sit next to someone for long enough, you like or dun like them . . . confirm have to talk at some point right? So over time, we talk lor! One day ah, I sit there talking with Hui Ting and Cheryl . . . I think to myself. Eh???? I quite like these people leh, and I think . . . I think they like me oso?? And you know what's funny? Most of the time Hui Ting speak to me in Chinese, and I reply Hui Ting with English. Or sometimes wif my broken Chinese. Or sometimes Hui Ting speak to me in English oso. When we still don't understand, Cheryl help us translate for each other! Then ah, got another Malay girl move to sit behind us also—her name is Rashida. She is so nice!! Slowly the group start to speak a bit more English. Even if the English is not perfect, the feeling of having friends is still a nice feeling you know? All of us, different race, different language, different culture, family at home oso different. But then ah, like magic like that la! Suddenly I can be myself, even though we are very different. I am enough for them.

(with a Canadian accent) But there were times I still felt like I stood out alone. It was my black, frizzy hair . . . my dark, blemished skin . . . and my wide curves that stood out. The boys in our school constantly had crushes on my friends and I was just always the girl the boys would want to talk about their crushes to. Nobody ever told me about having a crush on me?!

Probably because I didn't have the classic Chinese chiobu features that my friends have . . . you know . . . the straight, long hair . . . the fair, almost translucent skin . . . or the skinny body . . . tiny mouth, dainty lips, eyes the size of golf balls, and a button-sized nose. On many occasions, I would be with Hui Ting, Cheryl, and Rashida and teachers would stop us on our way to compliment them on how fair and pretty they were. Not all of us, just them. Even Rashida!

She was so fair, she looked more Chinese than I did! I would always be there trying hard to flex what my mother told me was a healthy sun-kissed, darker skin that was glowing from sebum overproduction, waiting for my turn to be complimented, but this is what I got from the other kids instead:

> KRIS *imitates the racist fucker kids that used to yell at her:*

RACIST KID: *(in Singlish)* "EH! Ah pu neh neh!!! AH PU NEH NEHHH! You Chinese ah pu neh neh! Why your skin so dark ah??? I thought you Chinese! Why your skin look like ah pu neh neh! Nanny nanny poo poo!!

KRIS: *(with a Canadian accent)* Have any of you heard this term before? Ah pu neh neh—it's a racist term Singaporeans use to refer to the darker-skinned people in Singapore. It's common to hear adults threaten misbehaving children: *(in Singlish)* "Eh you don't behave ah later the ah pu neh neh come and catch you at night." *(with a Canadian accent)* It's like equating darker-skinned people to the evil bogeyman. I might've had this racist term used against my dark skin before, but the few times I've experienced it is nothing compared to what the Indian people in Singapore have to endure daily. In Asia, there is value in having lighter skin. Whiteness is often connected to the idea of feminine beauty. The lighter, the better. Light is good, dark is bad. Fair is beautiful, dark skinned is less beautiful. Under the standards of beauty we live within, you could have the biggest, roundest eyes, the sharpest, daintiest nose and just the right sized lips but if you're a shade darker than whiteness, then it's like your beauty is second rated. When I was still a kid, a Chinese girl casually mentioned to me that she didn't think Indian people were beautiful, but that she thought Chindians were still alright. Okay let me explain what Chindian is: Chinese and Indian (like from India), mixed-race people. The reason she thought they were "still alright" is that she felt Chindians often have features that are the best of both worlds: the deep-set eyes, double eyelids, and sharp nose that a lot of Indian people have, but mixed with the light skin Chinese people usually have. My darker skin is only the beginning of how I looked different from the Chinese people around me. Puberty took me as far away as possible from what stereotypical Chinese beauty is. My hips widened out so far away from where they used to sit. And boobs. I was the first one in my class to have to wear a bra. Whenever we had to get dressed back into our uniforms after PE lessons, the girls in my class would always laugh at the bra I had to wear. I didn't just have boobs. I had . . . body hair. Think about the Asian women you see in the media: Lucy Liu, Constance Wu, Ali Wong. They're all light-skinned, lean and long, and hairless except for miles and miles of straight hair on their heads with no frizz . . . like a slippery eel . . . with legs.

(in Singlish) All the Chinese girls in my class got skinny legs. So skinny that when they pull their white socks up their legs, it can stay in a straight line one! But my socks not like that one, my one follow the curve shape of my leg. My friend ask me, “Why your socks stretch in such a weird shape one?” I hear already then I go home to try and straighten the shape of my socks. But the only way I can do that is if I use both my hands to grab all my skin and all flesh on my leg so there is only the shape of my bone. But when my hands let go, everything bounce back into the same round shape. I cannot make it go away. Got one time, this girl, she never even ask me, she just grab my arm and twist the flesh liddat. You can see the lumps on my arm?? The girl see my arm liddat then she say damn loudly to me, “Eeyer you see all the cellulite you have! So much! See? You do for me, I don't have.” Then all the girls, we take turns showing each other how much cellulite we have. Then I go home and when my mother was taking a nap, I quickly look through all her magazines, trying to see if got any quick tips on how to remove cellulite from my arm. I don't care if I got cellulite all over my body. I just don't want the cellulite on my arm to expose me. I know la, I'm only a kid. Children where got know what is cellulite one?? But I tell you ah, the other day my PE teacher dunno she bad mood or what. She point at the fattest boy in our class. His name is Tan Jun Kai. She said: “YOU. Do twenty push-ups.” Jun Kai was like, “Huuuh? Me? Only me?” In my heart I also like, “Huuuh?? Only him??” But my PE teacher said, “Yeah. Only you.”

So . . . he do push-ups in front of everyone. He cannot even do one . . . how to do twenty??? Some more . . . we have to watch him struggle. Then . . . the PE teacher say to the whole class, "You all can see how he struggling? You see his face so red, and so sweaty?? And then you can hear the sound he making?? Disgusting right?? That's how he look like when he's having sex! *(laughs cruelly)* If you dun want to look like this while having sex, don't be fat!" Everyone laugh, so I also laugh. If I don't laugh, later she do the same thing to me how?? I think she hate fat people. What if she punish me for having cellulite on my arms? I better punish myself before she punish me. I don't wanna look like him when I'm having sex!!

But . . . in Singapore everyone loves to eat. Budden hor also cannot be fat! Liddat then how, you tell me? You know somemore ah, even Wikipedia says that in Singapore, eating is a national pastime and that food is a national obsession. Eating good food brings fireworks of joy into any Singaporean's heart. You think I love to eat? Singapore loves eating even more than I do. So always got 24/7 flow of food, budden got pressure to be skinny. Not just to be not fat hor, but to be skinny. Before I move to Singapore, when I still in Calgary, my mom bring me to the doctor to make sure I'm healthy before we move. Doctor say I'm healthy and good to go! Budden ah, in Singapore, when she bring me to the doctor again . . . you know wat the doctor ask my mother anot?? WHY YOUR DAUGHTER SO FAT AH?! Den . . . my mother have to put me on diet! Can you imagine anot?! Xiao or what?!

Four-year-old already go diet?!?! I know you thinking I am not fat la or maybe you thinking . . . even if I am fat I am only a little bit fat but in Singapore ah the standard is NOT THE SAME OKAY. You know in Singapore on the first day of school ah, they weigh everyone in class . . . den one by one they read your weight to the whole class. Shame you . . . so no one will want to be overweight. You imagine lah . . . "Kris Teo! SIXTY-THREE KILOGRAMS!" Very pai seh one leh! Imagine is your first week of school, you still haven't make friend yet, but everyone know your weight already. Den ah . . . they also will read a list of everyone who is overweight and need to join the TAF *(pronounced tough)* club. T-A-F. Trim and Fit club! Dat means ah . . . during recess when everyone is eating and playing, the TAF club people running and running in circles in the school field while everyone in the canteen eating can watch them run. Very 丢脸one . . . I always scared because I usually got one of the higher numbers in class.

(with a Canadian accent) It didn't stop there. Two years ago, I went back to Singapore. I hadn't seen any of my family in two years. The first time I saw my grandmother during that trip, my family went out for some chicken rice. The first thing she said to me was, "Whaa 你好像胖了hor!" She told me I got fat. First words out of her mouth after two years of not seeing me. I KNOOOWWWWW, older Chinese people just talk that way, and they don't mean any harm, and she wasn't trying to hurt my feelings but woww my feelings were so hurt. I didn't speak throughout the entire meal. When you get told you're fat, how do you proceed to eat to your full heart's content right after? She must've known I was upset because halfway through the meal she said, "Krissy ah, 你很瘦。" Which means, Krissy, you

are so skinny. First, she said I got fat. Then she tells me I'm skinny. It's really confusing for my self-esteem. When I was in Singapore, I never missed my grandparents because I saw them all the time. My father's parents—Grandpa and Mama. My mother's parents—Gong Gong and Po Po. Whenever they heard me speak, they said I sounded like an ang mo because three out of four of them don't speak English. Only my grandpa could speak English. But he passed away when I was really young. He was the only one I could talk to. I still saw my other grandparents, but I only visited when my parents did. When I arrive at their house, I have to greet them. "Gong Gong!" "Po Po!" "Mama."

(switch to Singlish) If don't greet, they scold me. I won't understand it but my mother will tell me they are scolding me la. And I can hear the tone in their voice. I don't like being there because of how awkward I feel when I don't understand them. They don't speak English how can I understand? They cannot talk to me in English I also cannot talk to them in their dialect. I always just sit there and wait until I can go home. Sometimes when they ask me questions . . . even tho I understand, I am so uncomfortable that my mind go blank. Try to answer also cannot answer. My parents have to translate for me. When I am alone with them, I feel extra uncomfortable, no one there to translate for me. Scared they ask me questions I dun understand. The worst is when 婆婆 call my house and I am the unlucky one to pick up the phone.

KRIS picks up an imaginary phone.

(with a Canadian accent) Hello?

婆婆: *(in Cantonese)* Hallo? Lei mama hei dou ma?

KRIS: . . . huh??

婆婆: *(in Cantonese)* LEI MAMA HEI DOU MA??

> *KRIS holds the phone as far away from herself as her arm allows. Like it is lava and she cannot touch it or she might die.*

KRIS: *(with a Canadian accent)* MOOOOOOOOOOOOOOOOOM!!!!! THE PHONE!!!! PICK UP THE PHONE!!!!!!

I shouldn't have done that every time she called. I just found it so awkward that they're that kind of Chinese. The kind that can't speak English. She doesn't speak English and I don't speak Cantonese. How are we going to communicate? But now, only my Mama is alive and when people ask me about my grandparents, I know nothing about them. And that's my fault. When I look at other people with their grandparents, I feel jealous that they can talk to them, get to know them and laugh together. I regret that I never tried talking to them. I want to do better. I want to try harder. When people sound different from me or speak a different language, there's no need to be afraid. They are just people . . . like my grandparents. People who want to get to know me better. The next time I don't understand someone, I won't just ignore them.

I will . . . I will . . . I don't know what I will do but I won't just shut down on them. When I decided to move back to Calgary on my own, I thought that maybe people in Calgary wouldn't judge my body the way people in Singapore did. When I went to the mall for the first time, I didn't have to buy the largest size or worry if there were even sizes for me! And nobody would expect me to speak Chinese well! I thought Calgary would be the place I felt most like myself. But pretty much immediately after moving here, it felt like the people here already decided who I was and what I was like. One night I was out at a bar with a friend. Friends of friends of friends showed up too. I was the only Asian person in the group. Heck, I was the only person of colour. Two beers in:

STRANGER-DANGER BRYAN: You're cute.

KRIS:*(with a Canadian accent)* He thinks I'm cute! Thanks!

STRANGER-DANGER BRYAN: So, where ya from?

KRIS: Oh, I was born here!

STRANGER-DANGER BRYAN: Yeah, but where're you really from?

KRIS: My family is in Singapore, that's where I was raised.

STRANGER-DANGER BRYAN: Oh wow, so like you're Vietnamese or something. Sawadeekha!

KRIS is uncomfortable but she laughs anyway.

You're sooo sexy. Your tits are huge for an Asian chick. I know because I used to date one.

KRIS: Uhh . . . thank you?

STRANGER-DANGER BRYAN: So, like, have you ever dated a white guy?

KRIS: Um. No.

STRANGER-DANGER BRYAN: Did you move here from Asia to get some big dick?

KRIS: What???

STRANGER-DANGER BRYAN: Yeah, I bet you got a real tight—

Interrupt! Cut! Ah!

KRIS: OKAY NO!!!! What!?!?!?!? You guys were supposed to be polite!!!! AHHH!!! When guys talk to Asian women like that, how do they envision the conversation going?! It wasn't just tricky navigating conversations with boys here, it was hard to have normal conversations at all. With friends, teachers, bus drivers, people in general. When I met one of my very first friends in Canada, I thought she was great! She was always interested to hear about my life back in Singapore and was generally a nice human being. But once, I pronounced a word differently than she would've and she laughed and laughed and repeated the word I said while laughing over and over again. It stung, but I decided she didn't have bad intentions, and her laughing didn't mean she was laughing AT me. But when we hung out with other white people, she told them about it too. Everyone laughed some more. She even posted on Facebook about it. People online that I didn't even know had a great laugh about it. So I said, "Hey! I don't like it when you laugh at me like that. You understood me perfectly well, I just pronounce my words a little differently than you do. Making such a big deal out of it makes me feel ashamed about the way I speak." But she brushed me off and said, "It's just a joke!" This other time, she told me that when she got married, she would want me in her bridal party. Wow! What an honour! I didn't know our friendship was THAT important to her. Then . . . she told me she wanted me to stand up there with her because having an Asian person in her bridal party would make her look more cultured and well-travelled, compared to the all-white bridal parties her friends had. I would give her wedding a classy, international vibe. Plus, she said, I was a cool Asian! Not a weird fobby one. Which was . . . very nice of her. I mean . . . she was COMPLIMENTING me. It's a compliment. I can't shut down her friendship because she complimented me. I should feel grateful . . . right? Except, I don't. I just miss my family in Singapore. You know? I just want to go for a chilli crab meal with my family and eat till we can't eat anymore.

KRIS continues speaking in a Canadian accent but Singlish starts to leak in as KRIS gets more worked up.

In Chinese culture, and in a lot of other Asian cultures—food is love. When you are sick, your mom will cook for you. When families come together, they eat together. When you see your friends, you go to your favourite hawker centre and eat your favourite dishes. And everyone has their own favourite. So we all get a turn choosing where we eat. There is so much joy in food for me. So it really hurts my feelings and makes me so mad that when I moved here, people who are unfamiliar with my food *(switch to Singlish)* they describe my food as smelly!!! Then if it don't smell smelly to them, it looks disgusting to them. If you don't like then don't like la! Just say, *(switch to Canadian accent)* "I don't like it" or "It's not my cup of tea." *(switch to Singlish)* Why you have to say until like all the food I love look and smell like shit liddat. Another thing I seriously cannot tahan is when people here ah, they maybe never say any words, but they make a lot of sounds. "Eeeew-www" . . . "ughhhhh" or they make the face like I am forcing them to eat. Just gimme chance leh! I AM NOT FORCING YOU TO EAT. DON'T TREAT ME LIKE MY FOOD GONNA MAKE U DIE IF YOU SMELL IT LIDDAT! Dun forget hor! The food you are responding to is foreign and disgusting to you, budden to me, it is a way for me to experience love, home, friendship, and family when I miss it. Budden ah, sometimes, if I don't have energy for people to be offended with what I love, *(switch to Canadian accent)* I eat quinoa.

(Canadian accent) Mmmm, yum, quinoa.

GENERIC COLONIZER WHITE PERSON 2.0: KRIS. What are you eating?

KRIS: It's just quinoa, stir-fried with some red pepp— *(interruption)*

GENERIC COLONIZER WHITE PERSON 2.0: Your Chinese food is making me nauseous. I'm going to throw up.

KRIS: It's not Chinese food. It's literally just plain quinoa and some red— *(interruption)*

GENERIC COLONIZER WHITE PERSON 2.0: YOUR FOOD STINKS. You need to leave the room and eat it somewhere else.

> *KRIS has a durian with her. Like the real fruit. She has gloves, and a large knife like the durian seller uncles usually have. As she speaks, she chops and breaks apart the durian, first with the knife then moving on with her hands until she finally gets to the fruit. She eats as she talks. This is not meant to be pretty.*

KRIS: *(with a Canadian accent)* You think my plain quinoa is smelly? You have no idea what smelly is then. Smelly is when your public transit system will fine you with a thousand dollar ticket if you bring this fruit on the train. Smelly is when your dad won't kiss your mom for a day after she's had this fruit in her mouth. Smelly is when our production team can't bring in a real durian to the theatre for this show because the smell would linger for weeks. LITERALLY, WEEKS. That's smelly. I WOULD RATHER EAT THIS SMELLY ANY DAY than let you think I am smelly because I am Asian. And you know what? Those smells you find so smelly? I LOVE it. And, just so you know, I'm definitely the kind of Asian that slurps my noodles loudly while the soup splashes out of my slurping mouth! And! I'm the kind of Asian that stuffs my face with chicken feet and sucks on it noisily while magically manoeuvring the pieces in my mouth before spitting just the bones out. Yeah. My mother taught me well. Bet you can't do that.

Also, I'm the kind of Asian that eats the internal organs of pretty much any animal you can find on a farm! Pig's intestines, pig's ears, chicken blood, chicken gizzard, chicken liver, beef tripe . . . you name it, I'll eat it. And you better know how much I LOVE IT! And you know what??? I'm not just Asian, okay?? I am Chinese! Singaporean Chinese! And yeah! I have darker skin. And I love it! I've been sunburnt less than five times in my entire existence. And my mother is right. I DO have a healthy, sun-kissed glow. Also, I have curves! And I'm not ashamed to tell you that I love my curves. There's no need to question why my body is different in comparison to the stereotypical Asian bodies the media has branded into your perception. In fact, don't ask ANY questions about my body. *(switch to Singlish)* And aiya I don't care whether you think my English is right or wrong la okay??? You understand me can oredi what!! I tell you ah, I love Singlish. I love that I can only hear it when I fly home to Singapore. And actually with Singlish it's quicker for me to say how I feel. I'm not trying to offend you with my existence!

THE CHICKEN RICE UNCLE interrupts this outburst.

THE CHICKEN RICE UNCLE: 你的鸡饭好了！

KRIS snaps out of her anger.

KRIS: Oh . . .

She gets her chicken rice from THE CHICKEN RICE UNCLE. It is wrapped in brown paper, tied up with a red rubber band, and put in a plastic bag with dark soy sauce, ginger, chilli, and utensils thrown in.

KRIS: 谢谢 Uncle.

THE CHICKEN RICE UNCLE: 不用緊，不用緊。

KRIS takes her chicken rice out of a plastic bag and prepares to eat her meal. This is a swift and familiar process for KRIS. KRIS dives into her meal. The tension leaves her body and she feels like herself again. She sighs a big sigh.

KRIS: *(in Singlish)* Whhhhaaa shiok! . . . *(switch to Canadian accent)* Sorry I lost my temper there for a second, I just got really hangry. And tired. So tired of changing and adjusting and censoring myself all the time for the comfort of other people. I just want to be myself! What a luxury, to be yourself and be accepted for who you are. To have the way you look be accepted, to be looked at and thought of as beautiful, without needing to lighten your skin, or change your features or your body or the way you dress. I don't even need to be thought of as gorgeous. I just don't want to have to explain the way I look. Because when you get asked enough times where you're from, even if you have a piece of paper that says you belong, you start to question if you actually do. I dream of a day where no one comments about the language I speak or the accent I use, and that when I speak what's in my heart and on my mind, I am heard. I want to express myself however feels right in the moment. I want to be seen as a woman, a woman who is not just Asian, but Chinese . . . Singaporean Chinese. A woman who is smart, witty, and always passionate about what she does. A woman who is sensitive and cries a lot. A woman who has a good laugh that rises from the belly, that sometimes turns into a cackle. And I know . . . I am a woman who deeply enjoys eating a hearty meal. And snacks. And I also know . . . I am a woman who can be mean and bully others, especially when I feel insecure. I am a woman who has been treated like a fob in Canada, the same way I have treated others who were too cheena for me in Singapore. And I am working on it, because I am a woman who knows when I am in the wrong. I am a woman who values family. A woman who forges deep connections with people when they let me in. I am a woman who has lots of strong opinions but is also great at listening. I want to be known and seen fully as me—Teo Kris Vanessa Xin-En. Or ZHANG XIN-EN.

The lights go down.

ACKNOWLEDGEMENTS

My deepest gratitude to:

Mom, Dad, Keith, and Kristopher: Thank you for the unending love and support. Mom and Dad, you raised three theatre, culinary, and music artists in Singapore, which requires both balls of steel and a soft, mossy heart. Grateful to be your kid.

Swallow-a-Bicycle Theatre: Thank you for the serendipitous opportunity to seed the ideas of *GCL* in a cluster of trees while sparking sparklers, blowing bubbles, and rolling around in the grass. Back then I didn't realize SaB would be where I'd spend a significant amount of time learning to embody and practise my values of care as an artist, and I'm grateful I stuck around to evolve with you.

Jenna Rodgers: Gosh, obviously, thank you for your dramaturgy and direction, but mostly thank you for supporting the dreaming of artistic possibilities for *GCL*, for mentoring me as a bb artist, and for holding/empowering/nurturing me and my story over all these years. I am so lucky to be your friend and to be artmaking with you.

Thong Pei Qin: Thank you for your invaluable help in the translation and dramaturgy of the Singlish and Mandarin parts of the play, and for the giggles and guidance over my Mandarin pronunciation slipups and the generous "updating" of my Singlish knowledge. And I am so grateful for the warmest and most welcoming "first date" in Singapore.

Bianca Miranda: Thank you for generously offering your lived experience of existing in-between, for your voice in Tagalog during the early development of *GCL* when we couldn't find a Singlish and Mandarin-speaking actor, and for being such a supportive friend through all of this creative process.

Kiana Wu: Thank you liar/smiling Canadian shopper/sister/friend for listening and sharing your wisdom about the publishing processes, even from afar. And of course . . . for ur fraaaandship!!

Yelly Chuan: Thank you for listening to my story and translating it into this beautiful cover design. What a lovely way for our time apart to come full circle back to each other in this way.

Kris Vanessa Teo Xin-En (张欣恩) is a Singaporean Chinese settler based in Moh'kins'tsis, Treaty 7 territory // Calgary, Alberta. She moves between many roles, such as playwright, performer, director, producer, and Co-Artistic Director at Swallow-a-Bicycle Theatre. Kris's artistic curiosities come alive at the intersections of food, self-inquiry, and in-betweenness while working with a slow-cooked blend of care, anti-racist, and anti-oppressive values, inviting mutual presence and exploration. She moves, thinks, and writes slowly.